CENTENARY REN

OF

MONSIGNOR JAMES HORAN 1911 – 2011

WRITTEN, COMPILED AND EDITED

BY

TOM NEARY

FIRST EDITION 2011
Published by
Knock Publications

ISBN 13 9780951580776

British Library Cataloguing in Publication Data.
A catalogue record for this book is available from the British Library.

Printed in the Republic of Ireland by
The **Printworks,** Boyle, Co. Roscommon.

DEDICATION

This booklet is dedicated to the numerous people, at home in the West of Ireland and abroad, who supported Monsignor Horan, in various ways, in the implementation of his many projects at Knock. He was always particularly grateful to them for their financial help when he was building Knock Basilica and the Airport and for their splendid voluntary work at the time of the Papal Visit in 1979. He never forgot, either, the people in the various parishes where he served for their kindness, goodness and support at all times, those in Tiernea, Lettermullen, Tooreen and Cloonfad. He hoped that he did something for them in return that helped to lift their spirits and that brought a feeling of hope and confidence into their daily lives.

Front Cover photo: Liam Lyons, Westport.
Foreword photo: Siobhán Mallee.

FOREWORD

I am very happy to write a foreword for this book about my revered predecessor Monsignor James Horan on the centenary of his birth in 1911.

I was a Curate in Crimlin in the Parish of Parke in our Archdiocese of Tuam, when in 1977 Msgr. James invited me to assist with the organisation of the Solemn National Novena at Knock and the preparation of the Novena prayers and brochure. I continued to be involved with the Novena each year until my transfer to Tuam in 1985. Little did I know then that I would eventually be in Knock itself as Parish Priest.

It was during those years that I really got to know James Horan — the Pastor; the man of vision and action; the man of deep faith and spirituality; the role model for many priests at the time.

In 1977 James was in his mid sixties and he was in Knock for fourteen years at that time. He was in his prime and was already well into implementing his vision and dreams for his beloved Knock. It was very obvious to me that here was a man who knew his goals and aspired to them; he enunciated his principles and stuck to them; he set his objectives and worked for them with singleminded enthusiasm and commitment, and not just for the Shrine but for the Parish and its people as well, because Msgr. James passionately believed that a Pastor should become involved in the growth and development of the Parish at every level. He saw this as a natural corollary to his Liturgical and Pastoral ministry as a Parish Priest. In 1977 the Airport was yet only a dream.

When he became Parish Priest in 1973 Msgr. James realised that Knock as the National Marian Shrine had a great future. He knew that the Shrine required facilities and infrastructure so that people could have a memorable, prayerful, healing and peaceful pilgrimage to Our Lady's Shrine. I'm sure he thought that maybe the new Pope from Poland would come for the Centenary of the Apparition in 1979. If he didn't, he was often reminded of that possibility by the late Dame Judy Coyne.

And with breathtaking speed he spearheaded a programme of development at the Shrine and in Knock itself. To begin with he acquired acres of land; then St. Joseph's for invalid pilgrims; the Rest and Care Centre for welcome and hospitality; the first Confessional Chapel; the Blessed Sacrament Chapel; the development of Calvary Hill; St. Brigid's for the handmaids; the first Museum; then the "opus magnum" the Basilica; the first refurbishment of the Apparition Chapel; the highlighting of the Witnesses' graves; preliminary landscaping of the Shrine grounds; and in conjunction with the local people and Mayo Co. Council the development of Knock village. The story of the Airport is the 'stuff of legend' and that unimaginable achievement has already been well documented and celebrated.

It all was a tremendous achievement in a few years, but as he said himself he was in a hurry, and so he was. It is no wonder that it all took a toll on his health. Msgr. James realised that a lot of what he did was what we nowadays call "the first fixing". His successor, the late Msgr. Dominick Gealy, over the next sixteen years built on the foundations laid by his predecessor and provided many more much needed facilities and buildings in the Shrine Complex.

It was Msgr. James' deep faith and spirituality and absolute trust in Divine Providence and in Our Lady that sustained him throughout his life. I have clear memories of seeing him, after a busy day, walking around the ambulatory of the Basilica, praying the Rosary. He was a man who had a big heart and was noted for his hospitality. Sometimes he caused confusion in the Presbytery kitchen when he would announce at short notice that he had invited extra guests for lunch. He enjoyed company, good conversation, had a great sense of humour and an infectious laugh. I remember the banter and wit around the table at supper in the Priests' dining room in St. Mary's Hostel. The table could seat twenty and presiding at the top, the Monsignor could always hold his own. For relaxation, when he did relax he enjoyed playing a tune on his accordion and loved a good sing-song. And he was very competitive when he played a game of golf with his friends. Above all he loved God and Our Lady and he was a great and loyal Churchman.

The people of Knock remember James Horan for his many achievements, but they still remember him with affection as their devoted Pastor. He served them well and was part of their lives for twenty three years. He was kind to people who may have fallen on hard times; he was supportive to the elderly and the vulnerable; he often quietly sent members of the Shrine staff to do repairs on the homes of those who lived alone and felt isolated. In the words of the Prophet Ezekiel Msgr. James "looked for the lost one; brought back the stray; bandaged the wounded; made the weak strong and watched over those who were well and healthy." James Horan was indeed a Good Shepherd. And in the words of one of the songs in *A Wing and a Prayer*, the recent Musical celebrating his life and times he was ' A Man of the People '.

In the Summer of 1986 Msgr. James marked his 75th birthday and he celebrated the Golden Jubilee of his Ordination with family, parishioners and friends. In the last days of July, as the late Dame Judy Coyne so poignantly wrote in her memoirs "Monsignor Horan flew from his Airport again, this time to Lourdes, and as everybody knows, he did not see his homeward journey. In the twinkling of an eye, Our Lady called him to herself while he slept, for what must have been for him, the perfect homecoming".

And what a homecoming to Knock it was — his coffin the first to be flown into Knock Airport. So many people in Knock and indeed all over the country were shocked and upset at the Monsignor's unexpected death. I was privileged to be involved in the organisation of his Funeral Liturgy. He now lies in peace beside the Basilica of Our Lady Queen of Ireland, the building of which he presided over. I have no doubt that he is keeping a watchful eye on Knock Shrine and Knock Parish that he served so faithfully and so well for almost a quarter of a century. Ní bheidh a leithéid arís ann agus i measc na naomh go raibh sé.

I am delighted that our Chief Steward at Knock Shrine, Tom Neary has written this book to coincide with the centenary of Monsignor Horan's birth. Tom worked very closely with the Monsignor during his years in Knock. He travelled extensively with him all over the world. The Monsignor shared all his dreams and plans with Tom, who was his closest confidant.

Nobody is better equipped to write this biography than Tom Neary and I thank him sincerely for all his effort in doing so. And I also thank Tom for his most dedicated and loyal service to Knock Shrine for half a century.

This book is a most fitting addition to all the other publications about Knock that are in our Book Centre at the Shrine. It is the celebration of the life and achievements of Monsignor James Horan, the Parish Priest of Knock who will be remembered for generations to come.

Joseph Quinn, PP.,

Solemnity of the Annunciation,

25th March, 2011.

CENTENARY REMEMBRANCE OF MONSIGNOR JAMES HORAN (1911 – 2011)

I loved to mix with people in their daily lives. I loved to go into houses, sit down by the fire and have a chat. I knew and loved country people and I regarded myself as one of them. (words from his MEMOIRS).

When Monsignor Horan was alive and well and achieving great things he said to me one day: "It doesn't matter what fame you attain in this world because when you die people soon forget you and certainly after a few months you have faded from the scene and other events get the headlines". Of course, he had no interest in fame. His aim was to do, to achieve, so that he could make life better for people in various ways.

He really believed that but I would say that he was completely unaware of the importance of his achievements, his greatness and his talents. He preferred to call himself the simple, humble country Priest, the old man in a hurry. He is now gone from us for nearly a quarter of a century but his name still lives on in many parts of the world because of his uniqueness of character and indomitable spirit, against great odds. This year, the Centenary of his birth, is an admirable opportunity for all who admired this West of Ireland giant to remember him with affection and to celebrate his achievements. I have no doubt but that Monsignor James was the greatest West of Ireland figure since Michael Davitt, a man he always admired. After all, the foundation of the Land League and the land struggle coincided with the Apparition at Knock in 1879 and that date was a turning point in Irish history.

During the early decades of the last century the Horan family had serious concerns about land and it became the first major and social economic issue which exercised and occupied the thinking of the young James Horan. He had very definite views on the land question. When the landlords sold their estates to the Congested Districts' Board and the Land Commisssion, much reorganisation and transfer of land took place and it was a very complex issue indeed. When James Horan was a student, he helped to persuade farmers to give the Land Commission the property they owned so that the Commission could exchange land between farmers in the county and elsewhere. The result was that many families were transferred from where they lived to another area, including James's own family.

BIRTH IN TOOREEN, PARTRY AND EARLY EDUCATION.

Having worked with him, side by side, for twenty three years, as his closest right hand man, I feel confident that I know what made this man tick and I suppose I saw sides to his character that most people would not be aware of at all.

He was born in the village of Tooreen, Partry, Co. Mayo on the 5th May 1911 to Bartley Horan and Catherine, formerly Casey from a neighbouring village called Kilkieran. Bartley was a small farmer and tradesman – a carpenter and builder. He worked for the Congested Districts' Board and later worked for the Land Commission building houses.

James was the eldest in a family of seven – four girls and three boys. Their names were Mary, Margaret, Bridie, Nancy, Bartley, Pat and himself – James. Two other children died in infancy. He was educated at the local Primary School and while there he was lucky to have lived to fight another day. On his way home from school one afternoon he accidentally fell into a bog hole filled with water. Lucky for him another schoolboy pulled James out of the water and saved his life. The boy's name was Willie Hofmann and he was a German youngster. James never found out what became of him, in later life but he was always grateful to him for what he did. On that almost tragic day his school books in his little bag were totally destroyed and the ink from the colour pictures mingled with the acidic water of the bog hole.

From there he went on to St. Jarlath's College, Tuam, Co. Galway for his secondary education, having obtained a Scholarship. He often recalled how his uncle Patrick drove him to college, the very first day in a Model T Ford and gave him a present of a fountain pen. He was also treated to a circus in Tuam that night by his father and uncle and he really loved circuses.

ORDINATION AND SUBSEQUENT APPOINTMENTS

He entered St. Patrick's College, Maynooth in 1929 to become a priest for the Archdiocese of Tuam. He took Celtic Studies for his primary degree. He often said that if he had not gone on for the Church he would have been an engineer. During his years in Maynooth and even during the years before and after that, TB was rampant in Ireland. Many students in the college were victims of the disease and it was sad to see them there one day and the next day they were gone, never to be heard of again. Entire families were wiped out, in some cases. Of course penicillin was not discovered at that time. James was one of the lucky ones and so he continued and completed his studies successfully.

He was ordained in 1936 and his first appointment was in the Archdiocese of Glasgow, in the parish of Pollakshaws. Later, he served in Cardonald and finally in Dumbarton. He spent three years in Scotland and enjoyed them. He found the Scots very generous and helpful and always had pleasant memories of his time there. They were a jolly sociable people so he felt at home among them. It may seem strange that he had to go to Scotland but when he was ordained there was a surplus of priests in the Tuam Archdiocese, so many newly ordained priests had to go abroad for some time. He was one of seventy two ordained with him. He always had many memories of his years in Scotland. He recalled the rivalry that existed between the soccer teams – Celtic and Rangers and the hosts of young people on their bicycles going to Loch Lomond. He remembered, too, the numbers of Irish folk who had drink problems and who resorted to drinking what was known there as Red Biddy, akin to our own Poteen here in Ireland. He succeeded in getting many of them to take the Pledge and in time most of them became sober citizens.

MEMORIES OF THE KIRKENTILLOCK DISASTER

He had vivid memories also of the tragic deaths in a fire of ten teenage boys from Achill Island who were in Scotland 'Tato Picking' and who were living in primitive accommodation in a bothy on a farm near a place called Kirkentillock. Luckily, a group of girls in a nearby two-storey building escaped unharmed. He never forgot the sight of their ten coffins in front of the altar in Dumbarton Church for the Requiem Mass.

They were later taken home to Westport and were put on a train to Achill. The railway line that was out of use for some time was in operation that day and it was the last time that a train travelled on that line. It was said that that was the fulfilment of a prophecy that was made in regard to the Achill line. It said that coffins would be carried on the first train and the last train and that they would both be sad occasions. Twenty one coffins were carried on the first train and they were the corpses of those who were drowned in Clew Bay after a boat capsized. Those people had intended to travel on the very first train from Westport to Achill, but that was not to be.

Another problem he often talked about that existed in Scotland was that of mixed marriages as there was a good mixture of Catholics and Protestants there. The priests were reluctant to ask the Archbishop to get a dispensation for couples in those days and some parishes were more accommodating than others. If couples were not given dispensations they used to go to Gretna Green and get married in a Registry Office where they had to parade around a blacksmith's anvil. Presumably the guy there welded them together with the blacksmith's hammer. Some Protestants resolved the problem by becoming Catholics.

On his return to Ireland he spent a short time in the Franciscan Monastery, Ballyglunin, Co. Galway as Chaplain to the Franciscan Brothers. He was then sent to Tiernea and Lettermullen, Carraroe, Co. Galway where he was Curate. He spent most of the World War II years there. He often referred to the fact that Connemara people were always suspicious of strangers and they would be teachers, gardaí, public servants and even priests. They were, to use a Gaelic expression- daoine iontu féin – people in themselves. While serving there he had a health problem for a few months which arose from a burst appendix but he was back in action and in good health shortly afterwards.

While there he got the opportunity to visit the Aran Islands a couple of times to hear confessions when confirmations took place. He used to cycle the 36 miles from there to Galway and back again in the evening, a total of 72 miles in all. He eventually got his first car – a Ford Anglia. It was a real bargain at £139.00. Petrol- if you could get it- was one shilling and sixpence a gallon. There was rationing in force at that time. He also got his first house – a small one- which had to be refurbished.

His next appointment was to Tooreen, Ballyhaunis in the parish of Aghamore in 1944, not to be confused with the Tooreen of his birth. He ministered there for fourteen years. He ran a famous Ballroom at a time when there was need of some social facility for the people in rural areas. He even travelled to the U.S.A. to raise funds for it where Americans thought he was the spitting image of Bing Crosby in the film *Going My Way*. Back home, he got people to take electricity into their homes in Tooreen and procured a Post Office for the area. He helped the farmers with all kinds of projects such as building roads, group water schemes, drainage, land reclamation, reconstruction of houses, and he also built a Presbytery for £1,300. Sites were then £100.

The success of the Ballroom development, in particular, caused a certain amount of jealousy in the Aghamore portion of the parish and it was also of concern for other Ballroom proprietors whose business was affected by its popularity. They staged a hoax appearance of the Devil himself, in dancing mode, in Tooreen Ballroom, but it bore little fruit.

A view of the construction of Knock Basilica in the early 1970's with Monsignor Horan, P.P. and some of the workers on the project.
Photo: The Irish Press.

The Basilica of Our Lady Queen of Ireland taken shortly after its completion in 1976.

The scene in Knock Basilica during the Mass on the occasion of the celebration of the Shrine's Centenary – 15th August 1979. Present were 5 Cardinals, 24 Bishops, 200 priests, the President of Ireland, Dr. Patrick Hillery and his wife Maeve and thousands of pilgrims.

The helicopter carrying His Holiness, Pope John Paul II about to land on the eastern side of the Basilica in Knock – 30th September 1979.
Photo: D. Slater.

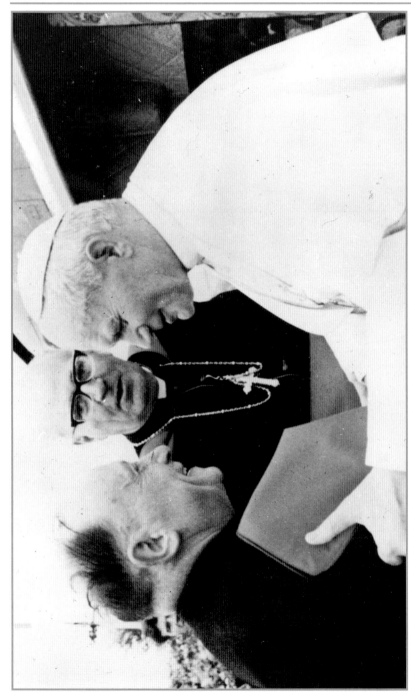

His Holiness, Pope John Paul II being welcomed to Knock by the Archbishop of Tuam,. Most Rev. Joseph Cunnane, D.D. and Rt. Rev. Msgr. James Horan, P.P., Knock – 30th September 1979.
Photo: A. Mari, Roma

View of a section of the vast gathering of well nigh half a million pilgrims at Knock for the Papal Visit – 30th September 1979.
Photo: Roscommon Herald.

His Holiness, Pope John Paul II in Knock Basilica in 1979, moving through the Sick and comforting them.

Photo: Roscommon Herald.

The outdoor altar that was specially constructed at Knock for the Papal Mass which was in progress when this picture was taken - 30th September 1979. Photo: D. Slater.

His Holiness, Pope John Paul II kneeling in prayer in the Apparition Chapel, Knock on the 30th September 1979- the Goal of his journey to Ireland.
Photo: The Irish Times.

A close-up of the Holy Father, Pope John Paul II lighting the Family Prayer candle within the Shrine at Knock – 30th September 1979. Photo: The Irish Times.

The Blessed Sacrament Chapel which Monsignor Horan had built especially for Exposition and which was blessed on the Feast of Corpus Christi - 2nd June 1983.

CLOONFAD – WHERE THE THREE COUNTIES MEET

His next appointment was to Cloonfad in 1959, where the three counties meet, Galway, Mayo and Roscommon. He had fifteen hundred acres of land planted there with evergreen trees and today they have matured into beautiful forests. He considered forestry to be the resource best suited to the area and it helped to provide a good deal of employment at a time when it was badly needed.There is no doubt but that he added greatly to the beauty of the environment in that area. As in other places where he served, he worked closely with his people and helped to solve their problems. He continued with his development projects of a similar nature, helping the farmers with drainage works and having by- roads repaired. His four years there are still bearing fruit. He lobbied politicians and procured Grants for the area as he made good use of all the State channels open to him such as the Minor Employment Scheme and the Rural Development Scheme to promote projects.

TO KNOCK AND ITS SHRINE WITH HIS DYNAMISM AND DETERMINATION

His next appointment was to Knock, Co. Mayo as Curate in 1963 and in 1967 he became Administrator. Then in 1973 he became Parish Priest and Monsignor also in the Seventies.

The Monsignor's contribution to Knock Shrine and the West of Ireland is now legendary. No other Westerner achieved so much in such a short time, against incredible odds. This Miracle Man was the right person, at the right time, in the right place. One could say that there was, as the late Dame Judy Coyne would remark, a Providence in it all. He had the skill to go out and acquire acres of land for future development, confront beaurocrats, at all levels, cut through red tape, refuse to take "No" for an answer and then blaze his own trail and solve problems that existed for umpteen years. He had drive, enthusiasm, determination, vision and a great deal of down–to–earth common sense. He could be as tough as nails when his back was to the wall but could also be as gentle as a lamb, in more relaxed situations.

The Monsignor often said to me: "When dealing with guys who think they know it all, it's most important to be a step ahead of them, two if possible and maybe even three steps ahead. In that way you can trip them up, demolish their arguments and win the day. I must say that anything he embarked upon was not without spending hours and hours of detailed preparation so that success would be guaranteed when it came to the crunch. It should be remembered also that he was a very methodical and organised person who always kept a Diary of his daily activities. That Diary was filled out every night before he went to his bed. The idea behind that was that he would not waste time wondering what to do the following day.

HIS STRENGTH CAME FROM HIS DEEP INNER FAITH

It should be remembered that the Monsignor was a man of strong Faith, of a solid spirituality. It was this Faith that gave him the dynamism that drove him to achieve worthwhile goals. In all the years that I knew him, he never neglected his prayer life, not even when he was under severe pressure. A great lover of Our Lady, many people often saw him walking through the Grounds at Knock Shrine with the Rosary Beads in his hand. Wherever he was travelling, he would have his chosen location for the celebration of Mass. I often accompanied him on trips and many times he would be reading his Breviary in the car and would then say the Rosary, irrespective of what time of night it was.

TRULY A MAN OF THE PEOPLE

The Monsignor did not allow any College course or any system to brainwash him or change him from his real self. It's true to say that he could walk with kings but never lost the common touch. He had an earthiness which was grounded in Mayo's country people and its various characters. They were the nearest and dearest to his heart. He was able to identify with them and could communicate with them. He was always on their side and the affection that he had for them made it easy for him to try to better their lot, in whatever way he could. That's the reason why they responded so well to him and he to them. He was always at his best among them. He felt that, as a people, they had been let down badly by all Governments and all political parties over a long period of time. They got lip service but little else, mere crumbs from the table. Political Parties spent their time tangling among themselves instead of getting together to do something worthwhile for the West of Ireland.

THE MONSIGNOR'S GREATEST LEGACY

When the Monsignor was working in Knock he would say that the people of the West had an inferiority complex and he wanted to change that. In due course he did, because he led them to believe in themselves and he gave them a feeling of confidence that they lacked prior to that. He instilled hope and a sense of worth in people so that they had the courage to get up and do things for themselves, in a positive manner. Morale was changed, changed utterly and they have not reverted to the old negativity ever since. Perhaps, that is the Monsignor's greatest legacy to the people of his beloved West.

THE MONSIGNOR'S SOCIABILITY

It is well known that he often acted as Master of Ceremonies at Concerts and Social Events and played the accordion to entertain the crowd. His father once told him that he had no ear for music and that he should give it up, but even in that case, he refused to take "No" for an answer. It was at Concerts and such like that he let his hair down, so to speak. It was then people could get a glimpse of another James Horan.

He did much of this work while the airport was being constructed, all over the country and it helped to bring in some funds to help bridge the gap. At that time there was what was called *The Monsignor Horan Road Show*. He was joined by a small group of local musicians who travelled with him to venues where people gathered to support the airport. Even before that they went to hospitals and nursing homes to entertain the patients around Christmas time.

He had a great humanity and sociability, not to mention his outstanding sense of humour which he would use to great effect after getting the better of some nasty bureaucratic opponent. His loud outburst of laughter was unique! I believe that it was his charismatic personality that made him so popular with people at home and abroad.

A LOVER OF IRISH CULTURE AND HERITAGE

It was no secret that he was a true Irishman at heart. He loved all things Irish, music, song and dance and had a large collection of LP's and Cassettes which he played in his car as he sped along from place to place. He was delighted that Sr. Martha, one of the Daughters of Charity in Knock decided to teach music to the children of the Parish, at his request. His love for Gaelic games meant much to him and he longed for the day that Mayo might win an All Ireland. This was one wish that was not fulfilled, however. He was a lover of the Irish language, not surprising, having been born in the shadows of a Gaeltacht area and of course when he was in Maynooth College, he graduated in Celtic Studies.

THE MONSIGNOR IN SWITCH – OFF MODE

Many people asked the following questions when the Monsignor was alive and well: did he ever relax and if he did what were his favourite pastimes? Not a few also asked: Had he any interest in sport? The answers to the questions are not difficult to give. Despite all the Monsignor's appearance of activity and high-powered performance, he was, deep down a very humble man with very simple tastes and interests. He was able to switch off from the work and to relax. He enjoyed the occasional game of golf but I never heard him say that he had a hole in one! Some of his happy moments were when he played golf one day with the great Christy O'Connor Senior.

He frequently watched the golf tournaments on television and after a long hard day he often sat in the armchair in his sitting room and followed snooker on the box. He had a great soft spot and much sympathy for the late Hurricane Higgins, as he was called. He loved to see him win. Was it the fact that he had an uphill struggle in life and to see him achieve, reminded him of his own situation?

Another of his interests was viewing the big international soccer and rugby matches. All of this gave him opportunities for expressing pride in his country especially when there was a win for Ireland. Sport apart, the child in him could be seen when he would stop off at a roadside shop and buy an ice cream or perhaps a bag of grapes and enjoy that luxury!

KNOCK BASILICA AND NUMEROUS OTHER PROJECTS

Having procured land for expansion at the Shrine he set to work. The Processional Square was developed and bus and car parks were provided for pilgrims. A Way of the Cross was put in place on the hill south of the Shrine and it is part of the processional route. He got Mayo County Council involved and the village of Knock was greatly enhanced. The rather ugly and unattractive souvenir stalls were removed from a number of locations. Over a number of years, the necessary buildings were erected. They include St. Joseph's Rest House, St. John's Rest-and-Care Centre for the Sick, Elderly and Handicapped, the Blessed Sacrament Chapel, a Confessional Chapel which preceded the present one and which is now the Prayer Chapel, a Museum, St. Brigid's for retired Handmaids, a Chapel at the site of the Apparition, the one that was there prior to the present Apparition Chapel.
He initiated a Book Service for pilgrims which has blossomed into a very important aspect of Knock, in recent years and has been expanded and

developed by his successors as the Religious Books' Centre.

He carried out a great landscaping project to beautify the place and he was very proud of the spacious lawns, numerous trees, shrubs and walkways but it was the building of the new Church, now the Basilica, begun in 1973, that was the greatest challenge.

At that time money was scarce, many people were unemployed and there was emigration too. However, he began his appeal for funds and the money kept coming in, from great and small. He sent out thousands and thousands of letters to people all over Ireland and beyond, even to friends of Knock in America. The response was generally positive. The new Church was completed in 1976 but before it was officially opened, a great downpour one Sunday afternoon forced it to be opened, prematurely, to shelter the thousands present even though it had no seating, no refurbishments of any kind, not even an altar but everyone improvised and it all worked out well. The date was the 16th May, the day of the Achonry Diocesan Pilgrimage led by Bishop James Fergus who had been Secretary to the second Commission of Enquiry in 1936. Present also were Capuchins from Dublin, Cork and Donegal. The great gathering broke into spontaneous song in the Ambulatory as the doors were thrown open.

It seemed to us that day that Our Lady of Knock had taken control of her new Church which was later dedicated to her under the title – the Church of Our Lady Queen of Ireland and it became the Basilica of Our Lady Queen of Ireland in 1979, covering one acre of land within its circle and providing shelter for 10,000 pilgrims.

HIS LIAISON WITH KNOCK PARISH

Despite the workload placed on him by the Shrine, he never neglected the people of Knock parish. He kept in touch with them and always moved to help them when the need arose. He had repairs carried out to rundown houses and he supported the rural community in all their projects. He enjoyed visiting their homes in the Autumn and the Spring for the Stations. He was with them in their joys and their sorrows and carried out his spiritual duties for them with zest and enthusiasm. He was very interested in the proper education of the children and encouraged them to learn Irish music, song and dance. He went on a School Tour with them every Summer to places such as Shannon, Galway, Sligo and Donegal, and even to Dublin to visit the Zoo and other places of interest. He helped travelling people and even set up a workshop where they made tinware for sale and the children attended the local Primary School.

The Processional Square, Knock with its beautiful flowers and the Apparition Chapel and Parish Church in the distance.

The Way of the Cross on the Hill at Knock which is also part of the Processional Route. The Rosary Procession here is led by the Statue of Our Lady of Knock.

St. Joseph's Rest House built to cater for the Sick and those with disabilities was run by the consecrated Handmaids of Our Lady of Knock for many years. In recent times it was run by the Hospitaller Order of St. John of God.

St. John's Rest and Care Centre at Knock which caters for the Sick who visit the Shrine for one day only.

Views of the landscaping in Our Lady's Domain at Knock Shrine.

Views of the landscaped Grounds at Knock Shrine.

The Basilica of Our Lady Queen of Ireland, Knock.

Monsignor James Horan with the Archbishop of Tuam, Most Rev. Joseph Cunnane welcoming His Holiness, Pope John Paul II on his arrival in Knock on Sunday, 30th September 1979.   Photo: A. Mari, Roma

The Prayer Guidance Centre, Knock, which was formerly a Confessional Chapel.

The Blessed Sacrament Chapel, Knock where Adoration takes place daily during the pilgrimage season.

Knock Museum which preserves The story of Knock and the major aspects of its history.

St. Brigid's which was built for retired Knock Handmaids.

The Pilgrims who travelled from Knock Airport on the Inaugural Flights in October 1985 pictured here outside St. Peter's Basilica, Rome with Knock Shrine Banner in the background. *Photo: Gioberti, Roma.*

Knock Shrine Stewards who travelled on the Inaugural Flights from Knock Airport in October 1985 with the Knock Shrine Banner in front of St. Peter's Basilica, Rome, with Most Rev. Dominick Conway, bishop of Elphin and Rt. Rev. Msgr. James Horan.
Photo: Gioberti, Roma.

His Holiness, Pope John Paul II welcoming Rt. Rev. Msgr. James Horan, P.P. ,Knock in the great Audience Hall in the Vatican in October 1985 on the occasion of the Inaugural Flights from Knock Airport to Rome.

Rt. Rev. Msgr. James Horan, P.P., Knock (Right) with (Left) Mr. Tom Neary, Chief Steward, Knock Shrine and (Centre) his wife, Carmel after the Audience with His Holiness in the Vatican.   *Photo: Gioberti, Roma.*

The pilgrimage group from Knock led by Monsignor James Horan, (Centre of second row from the front) pictured in Lourdes on the 31st July 1986 on the Eve of his death at the French shrine.

Photo: Viron, Lourdes

Monsignor James Horan's Grave which is on the Eastern Side of Knock Basilica.

The High Celtic Cross of Ahinny which marks the spot where His Holiness, Pope John Paul II celebrated Mass at Knock Shrine on the 30th September 1979.

The Inscription on Monsignor James Horan's Grave.

The Control Tower and Arrivals' Area, Ireland West Airport Knock

The new Kennedy Terminal (Departures Area) at Ireland West Airport Knock.

Interior of the new Kennedy Terminal at Ireland West Airport Knock

Display of Airport History and the bronze bust of its founder, Monsignor James Horan

KNOCK SHRINE CENTENARY AND PAPAL VISIT

Most people would not be aware of the existence of what is called the Knock Shrine Council. It consists of about a dozen Handmaids and Stewards of the Shrine who formulate policy for Knock Shrine together with the Parish Priest of Knock. It holds Meetings every year and a special Agenda is drawn up for each Meeting. It was at one of those Meetings that the idea of a Papal Visit to Knock was discussed, having been placed on the Agenda by the late Dame Judy Coyne.

The Monsignor wholeheartedly embraced the idea and lost no time in communicating with the Archbishop of Tuam, Dr. Joseph Cunnane, himself a native son of Knock. He was in agreement. From there it went to the Archbishop of Armagh and Primate of All Ireland, His Eminence, Cardinal Tomás Ó Fiaich. He was enthusiastic about the idea and he brought it to the Irish Bishops' Conference. Eventually, it got to the ears of the Papal Nuncio in Dublin and he forwarded the Invitation from the Archbishop of Tuam to Rome and the rest is history.

In 1979 – the Centenary Year of the Knock Apparition – there was much work to be done. Monsignor James had large attractive Plaques placed on all the graves of the witnesses of the Knock Apparition in the old cemetery in Knock and also on the grave of one of the witnesses who was buried in Bekan cemetery, a neighbouring parish. She was Catherine Murray, aged eight years and nine months.

He made a number of publicity trips, one of which was to the United States where he visited New York, Boston and Philadelphia, meeting journalists and speaking on radio stations. He also met three Cardinals while there – Portuguese Cardinal Madeiros in Boston, Polish Cardinal Krol in Philadelphia and American Cardinal Cooke in New York.

He also returned to Dumbarton in Scotland where he first worked as a priest after his ordination where he renewed his acquaintances with many priests and people he had known there. He also visited other places there such as Motherwell, Glasgow and Edinburgh, all the while promoting Knock Shrine and encouraging people to visit it. When there he met Cardinal Gordon Gray in Edinburgh, a man who visited Knock on a number of occasions.

A considerable amount of his time was taken up meeting people and dealing with the Media every year but the greatest demand on his time was in 1979. He was well aware of the importance of public relations. He coped admirably with it and I would say that he enjoyed it. One event that he often spoke of was his encounter with Gay Byrne on the *Late Late Show.*

Those with whom he had any dealing always remembered his great hospitality in his own presbytery. Nothing was spared to treat his guests in the best possible manner. He was convinced that this was a good way to win them over and to get them to help him out, in various ways.

As everyone should know, His Holiness, Pope John Paul II visited Ireland in 1979 – Knock's Centenary Year – arriving in Dublin on the 29th September where he celebrated Mass in the Phoenix Park. On the following day he travelled westwards, visiting Clonmacnois and Galway where he met the young people of Ireland and eventually arrived in Knock. Weather conditions at Knock on the 30th September were less than ideal. It was a grey misty and at times a wet day, very similar to the evening of the Apparition itself in 1879. It was not easy for the pilgrims who spent long hours of waiting, many of them through the previous night but there was an electric atmosphere especially when the Pope's helicopter flew low over the vast gathering before landing close to the Basilica.

It was a great moment when the Pope stepped out of the flying machine to be greeted by the Archbishop of Tuam, Most Rev. Joseph Cunnane and Monsignor Horan who said: *Céad Míle Fáilte Your Holiness! You're Welcome to Knock!* Pope John Paul replied with a smile: *Monsignor Horan, I Like Your Atmosphere!*

MOVING PAPAL CEREMONIES

His Holiness then ascended a ramp to the roof of the Basilica Ambulatory and did an impressive walk all the way around to the front of the Basilica , on the south side, in full view of the thousands assembled below him and stretching away from him in the distance. He was visibly moved, very emotional, shedding tears and gesturing to mothers with their babies and young children held upwards in their arms.

He then went inside where he met the Sick people in the Basilica, shook hands with many and addressed thousands of them in the Basilica and also the Shrine Handmaids and Stewards of the Knock Shrine Society before imparting his blessing. On his way out the south corridor of the Basilica he blessed numerous foundation stones for new churches.

His Holiness celebrated Mass at a specially erected Outdoor altar with the Bishops of Ireland and Monsignor Horan, gave a long Homily in which he said: "Here I am at the goal of my journey to Ireland, the Shrine of Our Lady at Knock". At the end of his Homily he consecrated Ireland and the Irish people to Mary Mother of the Church. He anointed some Sick people including Monsignor Horan's mother and the eighty-two year old son of Mary Byrne, a most important visionary of the Apparition at Knock. After Mass, the Pope raised the new Church to the status of Basilica and presented a Golden Rose as his own personal tribute and gift to the Shrine of Knock and also a large ornate Candle. His Blessing then rang out across the hills for about a half a million pilgrims present for this unique day.

His Holiness then went by Popemobile to the Apparition Chapel where he blessed the Statuary, knelt in prayer for some time and then lit a candle to Family Prayer at the Gable Wall.

After a cup of tea and a piece of apple pie in the Sacristy of the Parish Church, His Holiness travelled by Popemobile to the North Park where he boarded a large helicopter for his flight back to the Nunciature in Dublin's Phoenix Park. The crowds at Knock broke into song with pieces such as *We Wont Go home Until Morning*. It was then getting quite dark and when the helicopter got to Dublin it was not possible to land at the Nunciature owing to darkness so it landed instead at Dublin airport and the Holy Father was brought by road to the Phoenix Park.

The Pope's arrival at Knock was an hour late owing to the delay at the Galway event which had serious implications for Knock as the day progressed. The late arrival meant that by the time the ceremonies were at an end it was too dark to have the planned drive-about through the great gathering which was a disappointment for many. The darkness became a security issue. The up-side of this was that His Holiness got back to Dublin safely and that was of paramount importance. It was a difficult and dangerous time owing to the ongoing troubles in the North of Ireland.

Monsignor Horan's comment after the Papal visit was: *His Holiness was with us for three hours. It could have been three years, he was such a wonderful person. As a result of his visit Knock will never be the same again. Just because the Holy Father came here, thousands and thousands of pilgrims will want to come and pray here, to follow his example, to follow in his footsteps".*

When the vast gathering at Knock had slowly dispersed and the Shrine area was quiet and peaceful again, once could sense a strange new atmosphere. The Pope had gone but some way or another, his presence seemed to remain, especially at the Apparition Gable. As for the Shrine Grounds, after the event, souvenir hunters had taken away with them anything they could move, even the flowers and the shrubs and litter was everywhere.

CITATION FROM HIS PARISHIONERS

After the Papal Visit to Knock, the people of Knock Parish made a presentation to their Monsignor together with a Citation which clearly indicates the closeness that existed between him and his people:

"We the people of your flock, parishioners of Knock, make this presentation and address to you, our beloved pastor, to express publicly and convey to you our appreciation of, and gratitude for, your labours amongst us as our pastor.

"We are aware and proud of the recognition that has been accorded and the honours conferred upon you, nationwide and indeed worldwide, but tonight we turn off these highlights and concentrate on your sacred ministry in our parish of Knock, and who knows better than we the spiritual impact of that ministry. In spite of the many and heavy calls upon you from outside, we in the parish were never stinted of your help. You were with us in our joys and sorrows. Our material as well as our spiritual needs had your vigorous and effective help. The children, the old, the sick and the poor experienced your kindness and charity. All these ministrations were characterised by your own special brand of down-to-earth practicality and bluff, hearty good humour. Social life among us was enriched by your enthusiastic, talented and merry participation in all parish gatherings. May your bosca ceoil never go wheezy, your singing voice never lose its quality nor your ear its musical keenness. We look forward to more frequent renderings of your own verse compositions at our social gatherings.

"Service of God and the neighbour you have shown us as something happy and joyous. We pray to God through His Blessed Mother to reward you for your service to us as our parish priest, service to us in the spiritual and temporal spheres.

"May He preserve you in health and vigour with us for many years. To be aware of your greatness we have but to look about us in Knock today. But your crowning achievement was when you lead our Holy Father, Christ's Vicar on earth himself, to pray at our Apparition Gable. Memory of that will thrill every Knock person forever; an event second only to the Apparition itself.

"We bless you and rejoice with you for all this, but again we emphasise that tonight we want to regard you as our parish priest. With all your fame and honours, such an approach to a less humble and spiritual man might be off-

Monsignor Horan on the occasion of a visit to the proposed site for Knock Airport which he was determined to have constructed – 520 acres of bogland plateau.

Monsignor Horan in conversation with a local man at the proposed site for Knock Airport and pointing out to him the extensive nature of it.

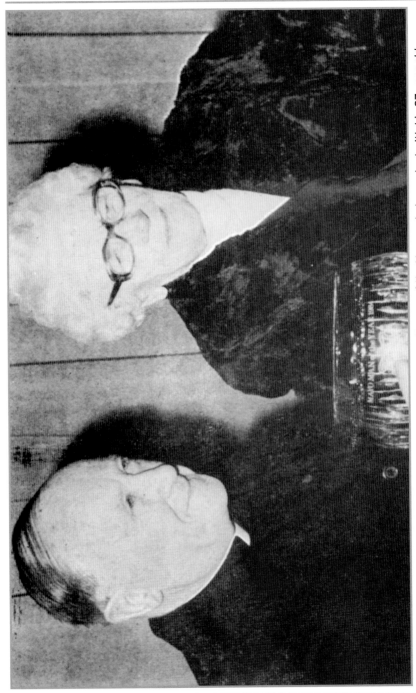

Monsignor Horan on the occasion of receiving the accolade – Mayo Person of the Year – photographed with his 97 year old mother, Catherine – 8th February 1985.

The Terminal Building at Knock Airport in the course of its construction in February 1985 with Monsignor Horan in the foreground.

The Runway of Knock Airport as it was in January 1985 being pointed out to onlookers by Monsignor Horan with a smile and a feeling of satisfaction after all the turmoil that accompanied its construction.

Monsignor Horan is presented with the first Charter passenger ticket from Knock Airport by Mr. Joe Walsh, Chairman, JWT (Joe Walsh Tours). (Not in picture).

A delighted Monsignor Horan waves goodbye as he departs for Rome on the day of the Inaugural Flights from Knock Airport – 25th October 1985.

The very first aircraft - an Aer Lingus Boeing 737 – the St. Eunan – to land and take off from Knock Airport for Chiampino Airport, Rome on the 25th October 1985, the day of the three Inaugural Flights to the Eternal City.

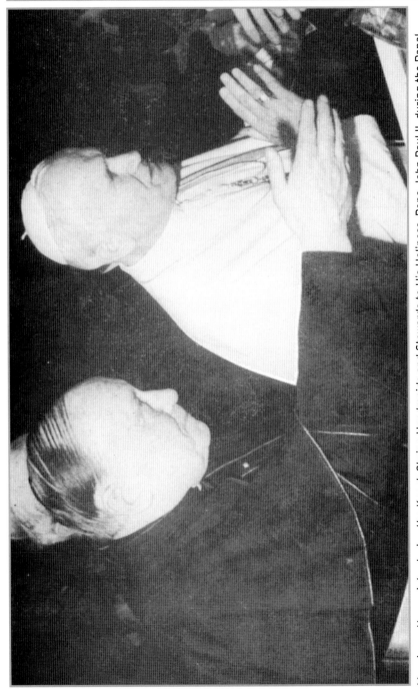

Monsignor Horan introducing the Knock Shrine Handmaids and Stewards to His Holiness, Pope John Paul II during the Papal Audience in the Vatican, celebrating the Golden Jubilee of Knock Shrine Society - 30th October 1985.

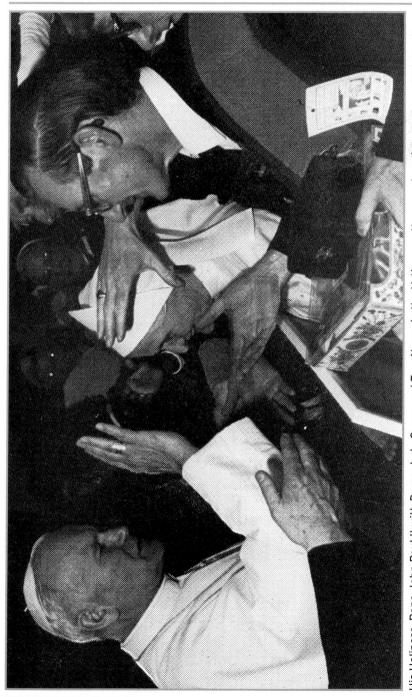

His Holiness, Pope John Paul II with Dame Judy Coyne and Tom Neary in the Vatican on the occasion of the Inaugural Flights from Knock Airport and the Golden Jubilee of Knock Shrine Society when gifts were presented to the Holy Father: A picture of Knock Shrine, a Stone from the Apparition Gable, Knock Holy Water and a book on the history of Co. Mayo -30 - 10 -1985.

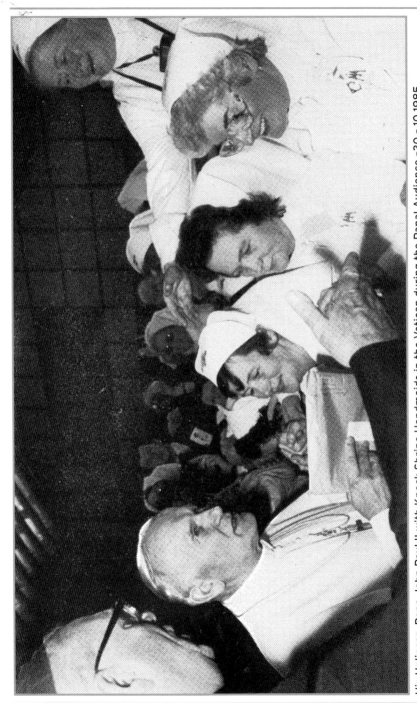

His Holiness, Pope John Paul II with Knock Shrine Handmaids in the Vatican during the Papal Audience –30 - 10 1985 . Nearest to the Holy Father is Mrs. Kathleen Reynolds, wife of Detective-Inspector Hubert Reynolds who was the Pope's bodyguard for his Irish visit in 1979.

On the occasion of the first pilgrimage to fly into Knock Airport from the U.S.A., Monsignor Horan welcomes the 250 strong contingent after arrival on the Transamerica jet with a pat on the head for the youngest passenger – 5 weeks old Thomas McHale – 29th July 1986.

A sad occasion: The ceremony at Knock Airport when the remains of Monsignor Horan arrived there on an Aer Lingus jet from Lourdes – 4th August 1986.

putting. We have no such disadvantage. Admiration and fame you have indeed gained but from us , your parishioners, something more precious – Love."

AN INTERNATIONAL AIRPORT FOR KNOCK AND THE WEST OF IRELAND

Shortly after the Papal Visit the Monsignor began talking about an airport for Knock. It seems that the visit brought home to him that it would have been very convenient to have an airport at the Shrine for special occasions and special important visitors. He had always been interested in airports and aeroplanes. He often visited Shannon and Dublin Airports and was fascinated by the flights coming in and going out.

He lost no time or opportunity to mention his desire for such a project to politicians and even to the Taoiseach of the day, Mr. Charles J. Haughey who in his own Presbytery in Knock gave a positive hint that he would support the idea. He with other leading politicians were in Knock for the funerals of two local members of the Gardaí who had been shot in Co. Roscommon by bank raiders associated with the IRA.

This was not the first time that an airport was on the cards for Knock. As far back as the early decades of the last century it came up at Meetings of Mayo Co. Council. It was mooted by the late Dame Judy Coyne and her husband Liam who were strong advocates of better transport for Knock and the West generally. Other attempts were made in the Sixties to have an airport built in Knock but it was not possible to procure a suitable site in the vicinity of the Shrine.

It took a man of the calibre of Monsignor Horan to bulldoze the obstacles and to make a breakthrough. He wanted an airport that would provide a warm welcome for pilgrims and tourists and he even envisaged having lovely turf fires burning there to cheer the visitors and a bit of Irish music to create the correct atmosphere. It would also have to be of a scale that would make it both viable and economic.

A small group of people who were interested in the project was brought together by the Monsignor to act as a Board to see the undertaking through. A Feasibility Study was commissioned and it recommended a number of sites from which the site of the Airport today was chosen. The land was bought from 27 owners for £200 an acre and every owner got one acre of Turbary also as there was much bogland there. It was a great expanse of plateau land, devoid of housing and relatively flat, 520 acres in total. It was procured for a nominal sum and the local people who owned property there were very cooperative.

Planning Permission was obtained on the 2nd December 1980. A flag was raised on the site on the 6th December and work began in January 1981. The first sod was turned in May 1981 by Transport Minister, Albert Reynolds. Present also was Minister of State, Padraig Flynn.

There was much deliberation with the Department of Transport in Dublin until finally agreement was reached on a number of issues including finance and the scale of the project. The sum of £8.5 million was pledged for the project at 1980 prices and the airport would have a 6,000ft. runway on which work began on the 1st July 1981. Contracts were signed the previous month.

The Monsignor was thinking in much larger terms than the beaurocrats but he refused to be down-graded. He was playing for a first-class international airport capable of taking the largest aircraft with a runway to match. He always maintained that a small airport capable of taking only very small planes could never be viable. He did not yield on that principle and eventually he got what he wanted.

He kept a line of communication open with the politicians, not that he would canonise any of them but to have them on side when he needed their assistance. His only interest in money was to get it so that he could do something with it for the betterment of people in the West of Ireland of whom he was proud, especially when he saw them working in their own region, either for themselves or for their neighbours. He used to say that they were long enough working for people in other countries.

The Contract for the construction of the airport was signed in June 1981 and it was given to a local firm – Mr. Patrick Harrington & Co. Ltd., Kilkelly, Co. Mayo. The actual construction work on the airport was spectacular. It began at the beginning of July of that year. A major drainage operation was completed and the bog that covered the area was removed. An access road was laid down also. The crooked was made straight and the rough was made plain. Truck loads of gravel and sand arrived on the site from nearby quarries and a solid foundation was laid.

In due course, the Terminal Building began to rise from the earth and the Apron gradually took shape. The runway seemed to go on forever and the ILS System was put in place as was the necessary lighting. Water and sewerage were put in place. As testimony to the ancientness of the site, a Wedge Tomb was uncovered beside the runway.

GOVERNMENT CHANGES AND MEDIA BASHING

While work was continuing on the airport there was much unrest in the country. There were Governments elected that had poor majorities so there were a few changes of Government in a short space of time. There was a General Election in 1981 and the result was that Fine Gael, Labour and Independents were in power. They allowed the project to continue.

A massive attack was mounted by the Media on the project which continued for a long time. It was negative, critical and destructive, nothing more or less than lying propaganda. Much of it was Dublin based. The airport became a political football also. It became an issue between the various political parties. There was the Barry Desmond outburst which could see no good in the project at all, a white elephant that would lose millions of pounds. How wrong he was!

A good deal of the dirt was thrown by little fellows sitting in their glass houses in Dublin, people who had never set foot in Knock or in the West of Ireland. Of course, they had no right at all to be dictating to Westerners as to what facilities they should or should not have They seemed to forget that West of Ireland people also paid their taxes and had a right to say, to what they were entitled.

Despite the love-hate relationship with the Media, the Monsignor saw it all as great publicity for the airport. The Airport Story was picked up by the world media and high-profile TV Programmes such as "60 Minutes" carried interviews with the Monsignor. What the media in Ireland missed was the importance of the socio-economic aspect of the project.

The Government axed the airport in December 1981 but that Coalition Government fell in 1982. It had left £4.5 million for the airport, to complete Phase One. An Action Committee was set up in Charlestown to help the situation. In February 1982 Fianna Fáil and Charles J. Haughey were back in power but were out of office again in November of that year. Some work resumed in that period. As no Union members were employed the Trades' Unions through their leaders were not happy with the situation.

The Coalition axed the airport for the second time on the 14th December 1983. Almost £10 million had been spent by now. The Coalition allowed that sum to the airport as a non-repayable Grant and that was it. Communications' Minister, Jim Mitchell did not amuse any Mayo people when he made his now famous *Foggy boggy Speech* in Galway relating to the airport.

Strange as it may seem, it was the Coalition Governments that actually delivered the money and not the Fianna Fáil Government who had supported the project from the start. As work progressed the runway had gone from 6,000ft. to 7,500ft and by 1985 it was 8,100ft. long. Its cost to date was £10.3 million. The changes in Government made the funding of the airport uncertain, but in the end the money came, in bits and pieces and it totalled about 10 million in the old currency.

AUSTRALIAN JOURNEY

As a result of the worldwide coverage of the airport and especially the Monsignor's interview on the CBS programme – "60 Minutes" he was invited to open an airport in Cairns, North Queensland, Australia at the time that work on the construction of Knock airport had been stopped, in the 1980's and he accepted the invitation. He travelled there in what was Spring in Ireland but Autumn in Queensland.

Cairns is in the Tropics and is very close to the Great Barrier Reef. It's a land of exotic animals, colourful birds and fish, with plenty of crocodiles and kangaroos in the wild. When it rains there, it actually pours, mainly at night, and the rainfall figures for there are quite high but the sunshine is glorious. Cairns is not unlike the West of Ireland because it is far from the seat of Government in Canberra, is off the beaten path and was often forgotten and neglected.

Many of the people there were Irish or descended from the original settlers in Australia and their Faith was strong and vibrant. Cairns is a Catholic Diocese where the Faith was pioneered by the Augustinians from Ireland.

At the opening of Cairns airport he met the heads of Government in Queensland and was photographed with the Premier, Bjelke-Petersen. He also met the Governor of Queensland, Sir James Ramsay. Not only did he open the airport for the people of Cairns, he also did publicity work for them with the Media as he visited various cities in Australia. He gave press, television and radio interviews and commented very favourably and positively on the journalists there.

The Australian journey was well worth the effort because it gave the Monsignor a much needed boost at a time when things were at a low ebb back home. The Irish media's attacks on his airport did some good, however, as they made Knock Shrine known all over this planet. He returned home via Hawaii and the U.S.A. and so completed a circuit of our amazing world.

THE GREAT JUMBO QUIZ SOLUTION, INAUGURAL FLIGHTS AND OFFICIAL OPENING

It was then that the Monsignor set up a small committee of which I myself was a member. Other members were: Marie Page, Jim Ryan and James O'Donoghue whose wife Mary gave much assistance with the work, as time went on. This small committee spearheaded a great drive to raise enough funds to complete the airport. A Jumbo Quiz was put in motion having huge prizes for the winners and in a short time this effort brought in about three and a half million pounds. That sum got the airport up and running. The Monsignor himself raised money through letters to friends of Knock at home and abroad and his successor did likewise shortly after he took over in Knock in 1986. A Church Gate collection which I organised with the Handmaids and Stewards raised almost a quarter of a million.

The inaugural flights from the airport took place on the 25th October 1985. There were three in all carrying over 400 passengers to Rome's Chiampino Airport – including the Monsignor himself. Travel was not a novelty for him for he had travelled widely throughout his life. The highlight of Rome was the Audience with Pope John Paul II in the Vatican . There were trips by coach also to San Giovanni, Loreto and Assisi. The return flights were on the 1st November – All Saints' Day. The official opening of the airport took place on a terribly wet day, 30th May 1986 by Charles J. Haughey who read out a piece of Verse specially composed for the occasion. For the Monsignor that day, a dream had come true and his investment in the project was immense, in many respects, but especially in terms of the effects it seemed to have on his health, though he would never admit that himself. Those of us who were close to him knew differently.

THE CHURCHFIELD PARK HOUSING SCHEME

During the time that the airport was being constructed the Monsignor was working on another project which was a Housing Scheme for people who would not be able to build or buy a house for themselves. His wish was that it would have a mixture of both young and old people and the young would help and protect the elderly. A low rent would be all they would have to pay.

He acquired some land in the Churchfield area near Knock for this purpose but he did not live to see the Scheme completed. His successor, Rt. Rev. Msgr. Dominick Grealy, P.P. decided to complete it and with the help of a small committee of Knock Stewards under the umbrella of the Knock Shrine

Association, a Government Grant was procured which enabled the Scheme to be finalised. Ever since, it's a useful non-profit making facility which has provided homely accommodation for many at low cost and it is only a short distance from Our Lady's Shrine. The environs are landscaped and peaceful and the houses themselves are attractive and comfortable.

HIS APPRECIATION OF THE SUPPORT OF HANDMAIDS AND STEWARDS

Throughout all the years that the Monsignor spent in Knock, he was deeply grateful for the support he got from the Handmaids and Stewards, at no time more than when he was trying to complete the work on the airport. He admired their dedication, loyalty and service to the Shrine, their generosity, self-giving and goodness and of course their love of the Church and the sincerity of their Faith in Mary of Knock and her Son, Jesus Christ, the Lamb of God.

A MAN PROUD OF HIS STAFF

The Monsignor always spoke in glowing terms of his Staff. He referred to them often and paid them compliments. He was proud of them and appreciated their loyalty and service. There was one person who stood out from all the rest and she was Marie Page. He put great trust in her and she helped him, in various ways, in the day to day running of the Knock complex. Her work included clerical, supervisory, financial, administrative, organisational and personnel roles. She was extremely loyal to him through all the years of his ministry in Knock and it is only right that her dedicated service should be recognised and remembered. As I write, Marie is still an employee of the Shrine.

HIS PASSING AT THE SHRINE OF LOURDES, FRANCE

The Monsignor went on pilgrimage to the Shrine of Lourdes in France on Wednesday 30th July 1986 and took with him his family members and the people who were closest to him at Knock Shrine. On the plane to Lourdes he spoke of his Memoirs, then unfinished and also about an account of the Airport that he intended to publish.

The pilgrims checked in at their hotel, had a meal and then went to the Shrine to take part in the Candlelight Rosary Procession. The next day he concelebrated Mass in the Church of the Seven Dolours and then went down to the Shrine for a Group Photograph. I did not think that he looked at all well. Later in the day he went back again to the Grotto and read the Office of the day. After that he returned to the hotel and had a rest for a while. When the ceremonies were over that Thursday night the pilgrims assembled in the lounge of the hotel for a sing-song which is a common practice in Lourdes. A man from Co. Armagh was at the piano and the Monsignor arrived, wearing a lovely báinín jumper, like the Clancy Brothers & Tommy Makem used to wear. He was in good form and launched into some of his favourite songs – *The Homes of Donegal, Moonlight in Mayo, The Mountains of Mourne, Red is the Rose, Galway Bay, He's Got the Whole World in his Hands* to mention but a small number of titles. His signature tune was sung in spirited fashion which was *If I Can Help Somebody* and the session came to an end at about 12.30 a.m. with the singing of *Auld Lang Syne*.

The Monsignor then returned to his hotel room and retired for the night but died suddenly in his sleep shortly after on Friday 1st August and for all those who were there with him at that time, including myself, there was an awareness that a great light had been extinguished for the West of Ireland and that an era had come to an end. There was a feeling of emptiness in the air. I suppose it was a very appropriate place in which to die, for such a man.

Many journalists came to Lourdes from Ireland when they heard of his passing and many of them who had frequently written about his projects shed tears when there – even the hard-headed among them. It demonstrated that whatever they may have said in print about the Airport, there was nothing personal in it. They were often only trying to get at politicians and political leaders.

His remains were taken from the hotel where he died and brought to the local hospital in the town and after a couple of days were taken to the airport out in Tarbes and placed on an Aer Lingus plane for the journey back to Knock. There was a concelebrated Mass for him at the Grotto in Lourdes and it was significant that the pilgrimage there at the time was from Scotland led by the bishop of Dunkeld, Most Rev. Dr. Vincent Paul Logan and he was the Chief Celebrant of the Mass - renewing the link with the country where he had first ministered shortly after he had been ordained in 1936. Bishop Logan retired recently having been Dunkeld's bishop for thirty years. His Cathedral- St. Andrew's - is in the City of Dundee. Mass was also celebrated for him in the Parish Church in Lourdes which is not in the Shrine Grounds but up in the town. The date was Monday 4th August. The Celebrant of that Mass was Fr. Pat Munroe of Cong, Co. Mayo, a second cousin of the Monsignor. Some of the journalists attended that Mass as did a choir consisting of pilgrims from

Ireland under the banner of Cuairteoirí le Muire and they sang beautifully during the liturgy.

His passing there will ever be a tangible link between Mary's two great complementary Shrines- Knock and Lourdes. Lourdes reminds us of Mary's Immaculate Conception. Knock reminds us of Mary's Assumption. It was because Mary was immaculately conceived that she merited the privilege of the Assumption. Both Dogmas are inseparable.

As one exits the High Stations of the Cross in Lourdes, there is a simple plaque reminding the pilgrims that Monsignor Horan, Parish Priest of Knock Shrine in Ireland died at that French Shrine on the 1ˢᵗ August 1986.

HOME WITH HIS PEOPLE

The Monsignor's remains were the first to be flown into the airport that was his brainchild and there is a little bit of history in that too. From there they were brought along the access road that he had built there and then on to the N17 to Knock, passed Shanvaghera Church where he had celebrated his last Mass on Irish soil. At Knock the crowds assembled to pay their tributes and on the following day the Basilica was thronged for his funeral Mass. His funeral Mass was celebrated by the Archbishop of Tuam, Most Rev. Dr. Joseph Cunnane with the Apostolic Nuncio, Archbishop Gaetano Alibrandi and His Eminence, Cardinal Tomás Ó Fiaich, Archbishop of Armagh and Primate of All Ireland, presiding. Many tributes were paid to the Monsignor following his demise. Archbishop Cunnane's tribute at the Mass included the following words: *He was a very human and good person, gentle and nice until he was crossed. Then he could be a tough man, and he needed all his toughness when tackling a project like the Connaught Regional Airport and seeing it through. He needed all his optimism and realism to face up to the opposition he got with the airport project.*

A former Taoiseach said of him: *He had a deep commitment to the people of the West of Ireland and knew what they wanted. He had a vision of what was needed there and what the people needed in terms of religious, economic and social development…. He was a brilliant and able man who liked a challenge.*

Handmaids and Stewards of Knock and the local Order of Malta provided a Guard of Honour after Mass. He was laid to rest outside the Basilica, on the eastern side where an impressive Celtic Cross marks his grave.

He had little time for himself because he was essentially a man for others. He was happiest when he was about their business. For me, his signature tune -

the Gospel Song - *IF I CAN HELP SOMEBODY* sums up his social dimension.

The composer of that song was Alma Bazel Androzzo who was born in Arizona, U.S.A. in 1912. It was composed in 1945 when she was living in Chicago.The song was made famous by the African-American Gospel Singer, Mahalia Jackson. Many singers made it their own such as Gracie Fields and Doris Day. It was brought to England by servicemen at the end of World War II, was published there and became a great hit song. The Irish tenor, Joseph Locke had a hit with it in 1951 and the Monsignor loved his rendering of it. The following are its Lyrics:

If I can help somebody as I pass along,
If I can cheer somebody with a word or song,
If I can show somebody that he's travelling wrong,
Then my living will not be in vain.

If I can do my duty as a good man ought,
If I can bring back beauty to a world up wrought,
If I can spread love's message that the Master taught,
Then my living will not be in vain.

The Monsignor's spiritual dimension is well contained in his favourite poem: I SEE HIS BLOOD UPON THE ROSE by Joseph Mary Plunkett (1887 – 1916), one of the Signatories of 1916. The lines of this poem remind us that everything in the world around us reminds us of the presence of some aspect of God. Its words are as follows:

I see his blood upon the rose
And in the stars the glory of his eyes.
His body gleams amid eternal snows,
His tears fall from the skies.

I see his face in every flower;
The thunder and the singing of the birds
Are but his voice - and carven by his power
Rocks are his written words.

All pathways by his feet are worn,
His strong heart stirs the ever beating sea,
His crown of thorns is twined with every thorn,
His Cross is every tree.

REMEMBRANCE AND GRATITUDE

May this year – the Centenary of his birth – be a time for rekindling his memories, for remembrance with gratitude. We are all very much in need of a glimmer of hope in these recessionary times and reflection on this man who gave such hope to his people in other dark days should be a great consolation and a true morale booster, for it is from the achievements of such an individual that we can gain the inspiration to press ahead with confidence and to conquer what may presently seem impossible. Monsignor James was the recipient of many awards in his day but my wish for him now is that he is enjoying the greatest award of all – eternal life in the presence of the Eucharistic Lamb and Mary of Knock whom he so lovingly served. Go néirí go geal leis i bParthas na nGrás!

The Inscription on the Monsignor's Grave reads:
In all our prayers to God the Father of Our Lord Jesus Christ, we thank him for you. (Col.1 – Verse 3).These words are taken from St. Paul's Letter to the Colossians and here it is appropriate to expand the quotation, from Verse 3 to Verse 6 with some adaptation, as one is not restricted here by a particular size of stone:

In all our prayers to God the Father of our Lord Jesus Christ, we thank him for you because we have heard of your faith in Christ Jesus and the love you bore toward all the saints – moved as you were by the hope held in store for you in Heaven. You heard of this hope through the message of truth, the Gospel …… which has borne fruit and has continued to grow…………

Some come this way but leave no trace,
While others build a lasting place.
Their footprints linger tales to tell,
Of all they did and did so well.

T.N.